# Horse Riding

First published in 2011
by Wayland

Wayland
338 Euston Road
London NW1 3BH

Wayland Australia
Level 17/207 Kent Street
Sydney, NSW 2000

Series Editor: Louise John
Editor: Katie Woolley
Design: D.R.ink
Consultant: Shirley Bickler
Photographer: Andy Crawford

A CIP catalogue record for this book is available
from the British Library.

ISBN 9780750264990

Printed in China

Wayland is a division of Hachette Children's Books,
an Hachette UK Company

www.hachette.co.uk

The Publisher and author would like to thank the staff and pupils at Riding for the Disabled Abingdon Group

# Contents

# Riding club

My name is Josh and today
I am going to riding club.

# Getting ready

I put on my jodhpurs, my riding boots and my club sweatshirt. Then I am ready to go!

## Top Tips

It is important to wear the right clothes when you go riding.

Mum is taking me today.
She will stay to watch
me ride.

# My friends

I go riding once a week after
school. I have cerebral palsy and
I go to a special riding club.

I love riding and meeting up with my friends there. They have cerebral palsy like me.

# choosing a hat

When we get to the stables, I have to choose a riding hat. My friends Sam and Enzo are choosing their riding hats, too.

Gwen comes to say hello to everybody. She is our riding teacher.

## Top Tips

Remember to wear a hat when you are horse riding. It will protect your head in case you fall.

# Warming up

Today I am riding Charlie.
Gwen helps me on and then
my helper, Lucy, leads me out.

She makes sure the stirrups are right for me.
Charlie and I warm up with a walk while
the others get on their horses.

# My helper

First of all, we are going to ride indoors. We all have helpers. Some helpers lead the horses and others walk beside us.

Lucy tells me to ride ahead as I am learning to ride on my own. I hope I will be able to trot on my own soon.

# Handy Pony Skills

After the warm-up, we go outside to practise our Handy Pony Skills. I have to steer Charlie between the cones.

We all have to go through the poles
and go around the obstacles.

# Collecting hoops

Then I have to collect a hoop
from the pole.

I tell Charlie to stop so
I can drop the hoop into
a bucket.

# Racing!

After we have practised our skills,
we have a race!

Everyone has fun in the races and
our mums and dads cheer us on.

# Mr Wolf

We sometimes end the lesson with a game. Today we are playing "What's the time, Mr Wolf?".

Gwen is the wolf. When she lifts her arms, you have to stop and stay very still. You are out if she sees you move!

# Pony knowledge

The lesson is nearly over. We all line up so that Gwen can test us on our pony knowledge.

"Does anyone know what this brush is called?" she asks.

I put my hand up to tell her.

# Gymkhana fun day

Gwen tells me I did well today with my Handy Pony Skills.

Soon it will be the Gymkhana Fun Day.
I want to enter the Handy Pony Skills
contest and win first place!

# Grooming

At the end of the lesson,
Gwen helps me get down.
She says I can help
to groom Charlie.

Then I take him back to his stable.
I give him some food and tell him
he has been a good boy.

# Going home

Now it is time to go home. Mum tells me
I rode really well today.

I tell my friend, Amelia, I will see her next week. We can't wait to come riding again!

**START READING** is a series of highly enjoyable books for beginner readers. **The books have been carefully graded to match the Book Bands widely used in schools.** This enables readers to be sure they choose books that match their own reading ability.

**Look out for the Band colour on the book in our Start Reading logo.**

The Bands are:

Pink Band 1A & 1B

Red Band 2

Yellow Band 3

Blue Band 4

Green Band 5

Orange Band 6

Turquoise Band 7

Purple Band 8

Gold Band 9

**START READING** books can be read independently or shared with an adult. They promote the enjoyment of reading through satisfying stories, plays and non-fiction narratives, which are supported by fun illustrations and photographs.

**Jillian Powell** has written many fiction and non-fiction books for children. She began writing stories when she was just four years old and she hasn't stopped since! She lives in a house beside a village church and still sits down to write every day.